# Mercy, Compassion, and Forgiveness

## A Prisoner's Transparent Path to Freedom

### CHRISTIAN MANN

**TEACH Services, Inc.**
PUBLISHING
www.TEACHServices.com • (800) 367-1844

World rights reserved. This book or any portion thereof may not be copied or reproduced in any form or manner whatever, except as provided by law, without the written permission of the publisher, except by a reviewer who may quote brief passages in a review.

The author assumes full responsibility for the accuracy of all facts and quotations as cited in this book. The opinions expressed in this book are the author's personal views and interpretations, and do not necessarily reflect those of the publisher.

This book is provided with the understanding that the publisher is not engaged in giving spiritual, legal, medical, or other professional advice. If authoritative advice is needed, the reader should seek the counsel of a competent professional.

---

Copyright © 2024 Christian Mann
Copyright © 2024 TEACH Services, Inc.
ISBN-13: 978-1-4796-1508-7 (Paperback)
ISBN-13: 978-1-4796-1509-4 (ePub)
Library of Congress Control Number: 2024910534

All Scripture quotations, unless otherwise indicated, are taken from New American Standard Bible®, Copyright © 1960, 1971, 1977, 1995 by The Lockman Foundation. All rights reserved.

Scripture quotations marked CSB are taken from The Christian Standard Bible. Copyright © 2017 by the Holman Bible Publishers. Used by permission. Christian Standard Bible®, and CSB® are federally registered trademarks of Holman Bible Publishers, all rights reserved.

Scripture quotations marked MEV are taken from The Holy Bible, Modern English Version. Copyright © 2014 by Military Bible Association. Published and distributed by Charisma House.

This book contains images generated by artificial intelligence.

Published by

> *"God willed to make known*
> *what is the riches of the glory*
> *of this mystery among the Gentiles,*
> *which is Christ in you, the hope of glory.*
> *We proclaim Him, admonishing every man*
> *and teaching every man with all wisdom,*
> *so that we may present every man complete in Christ.*
> *For this purpose also I labor,*
> *striving according to His power,*
> *which mightily works within me."*
> *Colossians 1:27–29*

# Table of Contents

*Acknowledgments* . . . . . . . . . . . . . . . . . . . . . . . . . . . *5*
*Introduction* . . . . . . . . . . . . . . . . . . . . . . . . . . . . . . *7*

Is Condemnation Your Strong Suit? . . . . . . . . . . . . . . 11
*Truthfulness* . . . . . . . . . . . . . . . . . . . . . . . . . . . . . *15*

I Am Righteous? . . . . . . . . . . . . . . . . . . . . . . . . . . 17
*Baby Steps* . . . . . . . . . . . . . . . . . . . . . . . . . . . . . *21*

Hope? For the Condemned? . . . . . . . . . . . . . . . . . . 23
*The Giver* . . . . . . . . . . . . . . . . . . . . . . . . . . . . . *27*

Is Your Faith Full? . . . . . . . . . . . . . . . . . . . . . . . . 29
*The Widow's Mite* . . . . . . . . . . . . . . . . . . . . . . . *33*

Am I Poor Enough? . . . . . . . . . . . . . . . . . . . . . . . 35
*My Love* . . . . . . . . . . . . . . . . . . . . . . . . . . . . . . *39*

Why Don't We Pray to Carl? . . . . . . . . . . . . . . . . . 41
*Knowledge* . . . . . . . . . . . . . . . . . . . . . . . . . . . . *45*

Am I Really a Felon? . . . . . . . . . . . . . . . . . . . . . . 47
*The Challenge* . . . . . . . . . . . . . . . . . . . . . . . . . . *51*

Pardon Me, Can You See? . . . . . . . . . . . . . . . . . . . 53
*Don't Worry I've Got This* . . . . . . . . . . . . . . . . . *57*

*Conclusion* . . . . . . . . . . . . . . . . . . . . . . . . . . . . *58*
*Appendix 1—The Gospel of Carl* . . . . . . . . . . . . . *60*
*Appendix 2—A Prisoner's Testimony* . . . . . . . . . . *61*
*Appendix 3—Prayer 101* . . . . . . . . . . . . . . . . . . *63*
*Bibliography* . . . . . . . . . . . . . . . . . . . . . . . . . . . *65*

# Acknowledgments

First, I thank You, Heavenly Father, for blessing me with an opportunity to honor You. You are my Strength and Salvation, my Rock, my Fortress, my Shield and Protector. I love you, Jesus. You changed my life when nothing and no one else could! Holy Spirit, how could I live without You? Thank You!

I dedicate this book to you, Mom and Dad. You have stood behind me through the worst storms and greatest disappointments. I pray my life honors you both from this point forward and brings you only joy and comfort through my walk with Jesus. Dad, thank you for showing me how to get back up and push through. Momma, thank you for showing me how Jesus loves me. I love you both.

# Introduction

> *One beauty of God's creation is this: if you're not willing to accept Christianity, then you're free to reject it. This freedom to make choices—even the freedom to reject truth—is what makes us moral creatures and enables each of us to choose our ultimate destiny.*
>
> Norman L. Geisler & Frank Turek, *I Don't Have Enough Faith to Be an Atheist*

This book is a gift. Every word has been earnestly prayed for and gallons of tears accompanied the compilation in your hands. If there is any virtue to any part of this book, God gets all the credit.

Whether you know me or not is of little consequence to me, but what I do care about is that you know who Jesus is. He has rescued me from myself. I was headed straight to hell with no intention of stopping. If it had been up to me, I would be buried in a graveyard and you would not be reading these words. Trust me; I tried to end my pain through suicide (that's another book) but God had other plans! I want you to meet Him and get to know Him as I have while living behind these prison walls. I may be behind physical walls, but it does not change the fact that all of us live in prisons of our own making; some just live under higher security than others, yet freedom is still possible.

If you are expecting to read a book written by a man who is perfect and who has never made a mistake, you might as well close this book now. I am not a highly educated theologian or a man who is esteemed by genteel society. I am one of the greatest sinners, shunned by people as a monster, hated by some in my own family, listed and registered as a criminal because of the terrible decisions I made. Nevertheless, I can assure you that if you have done things in your past of which you are deeply ashamed, you will want to keep reading, because you will come to understand the real value of transparency and the added importance of mercy, compassion, and forgiveness in your own life.

I am on the lowest rung of society's ladder of respectability. As I see it, moving up from the bottom toward personal freedom requires three major components: courage of the highest caliber, strength that holds on to hope, and honesty. Honesty can be the hardest of the three, because the exercise of honesty requires the other two—courage to be vulnerable, and strength to handle the consequences. However, I believe that transparency leads us to freedom.

By exposing our personal faults and weaknesses to the light, we no longer have to live in the darkness of guilt, condemnation, and shame. We can find freedom in forgiveness. If you are living with deep shame or guilt, I pray that this book both encourages and uplifts you.

Alternating between the chapters, you will read short exhortations I received over the years while living in prison. These are revelations, written in first person format as I heard them. All of these are beautiful gems that God poured into my spirit during seasons of deep heartache and suffering. Many nights, while humbly spending time in prayer at Jesus' feet, I was deeply impressed with powerful and encouraging words that moved my heart in ways which demonstrated God's great love. I quickly jumped up and wrote down everything that came to me.

I do not claim to speak for God, but only claim that I have tried to faithfully reproduce here what helped me get through my struggles. Over the years, I have re-read these simple words and great joy fills my heart with every reading. I find my spirit uplifted, knowing how much my Father loves me. I share them with you as a true treasure.

I pray you will find as personal a glimpse of His mercy, compassion, and forgiveness in these as I have. He has lavishly poured His love over me, a broken vessel, and is slowly restoring me back into His image. I love His tenderness, patience, and goodness.

Truthfully, the best part of being at rock bottom is that the only way to go is up! While you might not be down as low as I am, you may be able to find encouragement from a man who has found hope and is willing to be transparent. Maybe you, too, can find forgiveness for your mistakes and poor choices, and maybe you will learn to see others with greater mercy, compassion, and forgiveness when they are in need of those from you.

God bless you.

# Is Condemnation Your Strong Suit?

*It is the testimony of the Christian ages that the holiest men and women are invariably the most keenly aware of the humiliation they would suffer if others ever discovered the enormity of their moral failure.*

Dr. Robert S. Rayburn, Faith Presbyterian Church of Tacoma, Washington

I told my wife I loved her, but my actions spoke louder than words. One of my major failures in life was my unfaithfulness and lack of commitment to my marriage. I am ashamed to admit that I committed adultery many times throughout my eleven-year marriage. This does not include my unfaithfulness through viewing pornography and lusting after women as they walked by on the street. In this way, I was a terrible husband and a bad example to my two sons. To my wife's credit, or shame, she forgave me for the nine affairs that she discovered, but she filed for a divorce after my trial for sexually molesting my own teenage daughter from an earlier marriage.

> Yes, I am a criminal. I am serving twenty-five years for my terrible choices, and as a criminal I often wonder, *Can anyone forgive me?*

I know my action was much more serious than a mistake; it was criminal behavior. Yes, I am a criminal. I am serving twenty-five years for my terrible choices, and as a criminal I often wonder, *Can anyone forgive me?* I would expect you to feel anger toward me right now. Maybe you even feel like your anger is righteous and just. This is called righteous indignation.

It's interesting how Jesus handled sexual sin when confronted by church leaders who were filled with indignation toward a woman caught in adultery. His response was different from theirs. He hated the sin but loved the sinner, a perfect example of righteous indignation! Incredibly, He turned to the accusers and challenged their claim of righteousness, declaring, **"He who is without sin among you, let him be the first to throw a stone at her," (John 8:7).**

Notice who departed first; it was the oldest. Those who are mature in their faith are quicker to see their own faults and shortcomings. Eventually, all of the woman's accusers slipped out, with the youngest leaving last. Youthfulness contains pride, and pride harbors judgment—something I call *arrogant indignation*.

Cowering, the woman feels her shame. She knows her filthiness and waits for the hammer to drop. **"Woman, where are your accusers?" (John 8:10, MEV).** His voice is gentle and tender as He lifts her face from the floor, standing her up. She looks around in shock; everyone is gone except Jesus.

When Jesus is your defender, " 'No weapon that is formed against you will prosper; and every tongue that accuses you in judgment you will condemn. This is the heritage of the servants of the Lord, and their vindication is from Me,' declares the Lord" (Isa. 54:17). You might be thinking, "*Yeah, but you are a child molester. You are the worst, a real sinner!*" I hear you. My actions were atrocious, and I am *still* stunned by Jesus' words every time I read them, **"Wherefore I say to you,** *all* **manner of sin and blasphemy will be forgiven men" (Matt. 12:31a, paraphrased; italics mine).** Even terrible crimes like mine, which challenge our thresholds of tolerance, are forgiven.

I fall into the category of *one of the least of these* in today's society. As uncomfortable as some people are with my claim to be forgiven, their arrogant indignation does not change the fact that I qualify for God's forgiveness. I do not say that proudly. It is forever with great sadness that I must admit my past sins, yet transparency leads us to freedom.

I wonder, are *you* unwilling to forgive? Those we consider the worst of sinners must be treated with mercy, compassion, and forgiveness if we expect to receive the same. Jesus said, **"Do not judge so that you will not be judged. For in the way you judge, you will be judged; and by your standard of measure, it will be measured to you" (Matt. 7:1–2).** That statement jolts me to the core every time I read it.

There is a secret I have learned, an antidote against judgmentalism. It has given me great freedom, built spiritual maturity, and brought healing. It is simple and yet profound: confession. **"Therefore, confess your sins to one another, and pray for one another so that you may be healed. The effective prayer of a righteous man can accomplish much" (James 5:16).** Think about it. What if we came to church and really opened up to each other? What if after that, we prayed for each other and fostered forgiveness in our hearts toward each other for our many slip-ups and shortcomings? I bet this would be quite transformative! If we stopped *playing* church and became a *praying* church, I bet we would we find more mercy, compassion, and forgiveness!

Actions speak louder than words, and open-hearted, loving prayer for the one who confesses his failures proclaims, "I love you!"

*Father, I confess, I have fallen short in my actions toward others. I use my words to condemn others while at the same time I ask You for mercy. I see my condition and I desperately need Your compassion. Make me more like Jesus, forgiving others. Help me to say, "Neither do I condemn you, go and sin no more." In Jesus' name, amen.*

# Truthfulness

## *An Exhortation from Jesus*

Truthfulness is a defining characteristic of being one of My followers. This is a foundational pillar easily ignored and discounted. Little lies, commonly known as "white lies," are justified and condoned even by those who claim to follow Me. I am *not* the Father of lies. I am the Way, the **Truth,** and the Life. It takes real courage to become a truth teller. True Christians are the most courageous people on Earth when they resist lying and denounce this subtle temptation. The enemy, Satan, is a crafty liar. He convinces many believers to take the easy way out and cover up or distort the truth.

He says, *"You don't have to expose yourself like that."*

I created your mind to form habits. By lying, your habits will lead you to distorted thinking, a thinking that accepts lying as normal. I am telling you that this path is especially dangerous, because eventually it leads you to lie to yourself. Many sincere Christians have turned away from Me because of this self-deception. They no longer feel true humility or a need to repent of sin. Many Christians say that they are saved, but they are deceived and will be lost, if they do not turn fully to Me in truth and admit their need of Me. The world is in need of truth tellers, men and women who will stand truthfully in life, business, marriage, and in faith. These truthful people will stand tall against a backdrop of selfishness, sinfulness, and worldliness, which the world accepts as okay.

Will you tell the truth for Me? Will you deny this world and all that the world considers to be truth in the eyes of people? What if you were to declare boldly that I am the Truth? I honor those who honor Me. My Word is truth. My promises are true. Follow Me. I have set the standard of truth and raised it for all to see. By your courage, others will see it too.

# I Am Righteous?

*If the lost and suffering people of this world only knew what a perfect Father our God is—if they only realized the inheritance He has planned as a gift— then they would be far more likely to accept the privilege of becoming His child.*

Danny Shelton, *The Ten Commandments Twice Removed*

In prison, life is hard. Access to everything is limited and inmates can only move from one area to another during specified times. Our captors exercise total control at all times, and roving checks ensure that we have not tried to escape and are all still accounted for.

However, despite the heavy security, a single guard has the ability and authority to escort an inmate anywhere within the facility at any time. The only thing the guard has to say is, "He is with me," and access becomes available to the inmate. In the same way, God's children (the inmates of this sinful world) will one day get an escort to a new home when Jesus says to His Father, *"They are with Me!"*

Remember the prodigal son? He was a rebellious son who felt trapped in his father's house. He decided that he would be better off alone. He hated the rules and restrictions that kept him from what he considered true freedom. He confronted his father and said, "Give me my half of the inheritance now." His father gave him what he asked for and the son left his home with the money.

He ended up in a faraway country where he knew that nobody would know his father. He made new friends and soon was very popular in the city. Boy, did he have fun! He partied and drank, and paid the tab so that everyone had a good time with him. He was sure that all of his new friends really loved him, until his money ran out. Suddenly, everyone abandoned him. He found himself homeless and very hungry. He got a job working on a pig farm and before long the pigs' food started to look appetizing!

The Bible says that when this rebellious son saw his condition, "he came to his senses" (Luke 15:17). You see, all that time when he was out partying and philandering, he was not in his right mind; but when he hit bottom, reality struck and he came to his senses.

Maybe you have lost everything: family, friends, money, your house, your job, even your dignity. You have hit bottom. At my lowest point, I attempted suicide. Only by God's mercy did I survive. It was then that I came to my senses. I realized my utter helplessness and need of Jesus. I came to see that He must have a purpose for my life. I wonder, *Why is it that so many of us have to lose it all before we understand what we have lost?*

The rebellious son thought about his father at that moment while he was looking at the pig slop. *My father treats his own servants better than I'm being treated right now; at least they have bread to eat and here I am starving. You know what? I'm going to go back and tell father that I made a mistake. I know that I am not worthy of being a son anymore, but I will work for him as a hired man. At least then I know that I will be able to eat!* This was the son's point of transparency. He reached a place of full surrender, rather than pride and stubbornness. There is freedom there, my friends!

What this young man had never realized was who his father was! How could he have known that every day while he was gone, his father had been looking for him, waiting for his son to appear over the horizon? Imagine the son's shock as he sees his dignified father running, holding up his robe, exposing his legs, shamelessly throwing aside his dignity and sprinting to him, the unworthy son in his pig-smelling clothes.

He was the same son who had publicly shamed his father, rejected him, and selfishly demanded his own way. He was the same son who had squandered all of his inheritance, yet his father sees none of that now. He sees his son! He is cheering jubilantly, "He was *lost* but now he is *found!*" His father is now embracing him; joy is beaming from his face. People are watching, shocked, stunned at the sight, repulsed by the smell of this found son.

Now the father speaks with authority. He is a powerful, wealthy landowner. His orders *will* be followed and carried out at once! "Quickly bring out the best robe and put it on him" (verse 22). The Father's robe covers the shame of his son's filthy rags. In the same way, Jesus puts a robe over us and covers our sinfulness. This is called His robe of righteousness. What amazing grace!

Next comes the Father's command, "Put a ring on his hand"(ibid.). In this moment, he restores his son's signet authority to sign for business in the family's name (the father's name!). All of the father's wealth is fully available at the son's request! Then the father says something incredible, "Put … sandals on his feet" (ibid.). Everyone knows that servants do not wear sandals; sons wear sandals! What beautiful restorative mercy, compassion, and forgiveness!

The father, *our* Father, is saying, *"He is with Me. I have made him righteous."* Wow! Maybe like me you have been an undeserving child and hit bottom—but your heavenly Father is eagerly waiting for you to come back home so He can restore you to the family.

One day soon He will come back to this earth, gloriously filling up the sky with the splendor of Heaven surrounding Him. Bursting from Heaven, brighter than the noonday sun, He will gather His sons and daughters and escort them home. Then Jesus will say, *"Father, I desire that they ... be with Me"* (John 17:24). How wonderful it is to know that in Christ we are righteous and have access to heaven. He desires for us to live forever under the gift of His mercy, compassion, and forgiveness.

*Father, thank You for desiring us—Your wretched, rebellious, ungrateful, runaway children. Help us to quickly come to our senses and see our righteousness in Christ. Help us to know that Your desire is to say, "They are with Me." Thank You for amazing grace. Amen.*

# Baby Steps

*From Your Father, with Love*

Do you remember your first steps in life? Maybe you remember the first steps your children took. Did they fall down the first few times? Did you yell at them and tell them that they were worthless because of it?

No!

Why do you think that I am any different?

When you fall, I am watching. I always run to help pick you back up and place you on your feet again. I praise you for every step you take toward Me and I wrap you in a warm and loving embrace when you get tired. You know that I rejoice over you, don't you? I am proud to be your Father, and your successes are celebrated.

Did you ever get into an accident? What was the first question that all of your friends asked you when they found out about it? *"Are you OK?"*

I am like that!

I am not a bully. When you fell off your bike as a kid and skinned your knee, did your parents push you back down and cause you to skin the other one? Of course not! They cleaned the wound, wiped your tears, and gave you a Band-Aid®.

I am like that!

When you fell down, I gave you Jesus. He blots out your sins and heals your wounds. You do not need to feel shame or embarrassment when you come to Me. As a child, were you embarrassed to run to someone who loved you when you were hurt or had fallen? No! You ran to them crying, knowing that they would help you and make it all better. This is what I mean by telling you to become like a little child. Perfect love casts out all fear. My love is perfect and it takes away fear! You can run to Me.

Maybe you did not feel loved as a child, or maybe those who were supposed to be your protectors were hurtful to you. These are not good examples of my love. They hurt you because they had been hurt, too. I am sorry that they treated you this way. I am not like them. I cherish you and I am always going to treat you with kindness and tenderness. I cannot wait for you to get home. I am waiting on the doorstep to run to you and embrace you. You are My beloved child, and I will forever be your loving Father.

# Hope? For the Condemned?

*Please do not allow yourself to lose your trust in the Lord by thinking that perhaps you are somehow deficient in your spiritual life, and therefore unable to draw closer to Him. Take courage.*

Roger Morneau, *When You Need Incredible Answers to Prayer*

The other day I sat down and completely read the transcript of my trial, as well as the statements written by my wife and daughter. The pain and agony in their words, written from a place of brokenness and loss, pierced my heart to the core as I read them. I have had years to reflect on my terrible behavior, and when I look back I see a man who was arrogant, proud, selfish, and stubborn. In my quiet moments, I kick myself for my own stupidity and stubbornness. To put it bluntly, I feel shame. This is called self-condemnation.

Looking back over the course of my life, I can see the devastation left in the wake of my choices. Without a doubt, my actions have hurt and ruined relationships, some of which may never recover. To admit this hurts me deeply, because I never thought that I would do such things.

> "What if I am living under self-condemnation and despair right now?" The good news is that there is a way out of self-condemnation for you today.

I have talked to men in prison who will not forgive themselves for what they have done. They are broken shells of the men they once were, and they live under constant self-condemnation. While it is healthy to acknowledge the pain and suffering your actions have brought to others (this pain runs very deep because of my horrible behavior) eventually forgiveness must come if restoration is desired. We cannot control the forgiveness of others, but we *can* control forgiveness of ourselves. Just as a physical wound takes time, *physical* therapy, and exercise to heal, so forgiveness takes time, *emotional* therapy, and the exercise of forgiving others and ourselves. Yes, scars may remain, but those scars remind us of what we have been through, and how we have healed.

Some say, "That is good and all, but what about today? What if I am living under self-condemnation and despair right now?" The good news is that there is a way out of self-condemnation for you today.

STEP ONE requires a look in the mirror. Ask yourself, *Is there anyone that I am judging or condemning right now?* Jesus said, **"Do not judge, and you will not be judged; and do not condemn, and you will not be condemned; pardon, and you will be pardoned" (Luke 6:37).** When we approach God for release from self-condemnation, we first need to be willing to release the condemnation we hold against others. This is one way we keep God's commandment of loving our neighbor as ourselves.

STEP TWO is confession. *Lay your sins before Jesus* and trust that He has forgiven you. **"If we confess our sins, He is faithful and righteous to forgive us our sins and to cleanse us from all unrighteousness" (1 John 1:9).** Remember, transparency leads us to freedom. **"Therefore there is now no condemnation for those who are in Christ Jesus. For the law of the Spirit of life in Christ Jesus has set you free from the law of sin and of death" (Rom. 8:1–2).** This is so powerful!

STEP THREE, believe what you have read and speak it out loud over your life, "*I accept that You have done this for me, Jesus.* There is now no condemnation over my life because You have set me free. Thank You!" If you have followed and believed what these verses said, you are now free! This is great news. Believe it!

Did you know that Jesus became sin, so that you could become righteous? Look it up for yourself. In 2 Corinthians 5:21 it says, **"He [God] made Him [Jesus] who knew no sin to be sin on our behalf, so that we might become the righteousness of God in Him."** Wow! Now *that* is good news! That is worth shouting out loud over, isn't it?

Even non-Christians have heard that Jesus died for their sins; that is the common gospel preached from every street corner. But why do most Christians leave out the best part? Why do most Christians neglect the fact that, in Christ, they *become righteous*? I believe the reason is that most people, Christians included, are filled with self-condemnation. We tell ourselves that we are not worthy of righteousness because of our sins, but we just read that Jesus became sin for us!

The question you must ask yourself is *Do I really believe it? Is God's grace bigger than my sin?* Paul seemed to think so, **"But where sin increased, grace abounded all the more" (Rom. 5:20). "But now having been freed from sin … you derive your benefit, resulting in sanctification, and the outcome, eternal life" (Rom. 6:22).**

Someday, we will all look with wonder at the scars on the hands and feet of Jesus, pierced because of our sins. We will see His back and side—where He was whipped, beaten, and stabbed, so that we could live with Him without pain. He will tell us about the ropes that wicked men used to bind His hands, hands that had only brought healing, so we could be free. We will stare in awe at

His forehead, where the crown of thorns tore into his tender brow so that we could wear a golden crown of glory.

Then, realizing the wonderful extent of His love, we will throw our glittering crowns at His holy feet and cry, **"Worthy is the Lamb that was slain to receive power and riches and wisdom and might and honor and glory and blessing" (Rev. 5:12).** After ten thousand years, this same story will be sweeter, richer, and deeper in meaning to us than ever before. The ones who were condemned, worthy of death, and without hope, will then say, *"I am righteous because of Jesus."* We will never tire of this beautiful story, and we will never cease to marvel at the majesty of our incredible King who humbled Himself for us. What unspeakable love! What indescribable mercy, compassion, and forgiveness!

As I survey the wreck of my life, I honestly admit my own deep failures. Fortunately, that is not where my story ends. In Christ, I am righteous. Unbelievable? Yes, almost; but I choose to believe that God's power and grace are greater than my deepest sin. I pray that you, too, find hope in Jesus and say with me, "I am no longer condemned. I have been set free!"

*Jesus, all of this seems almost too good to be true, but I know that You are not a liar. I accept Your gift of righteousness in place of my self-condemnation. I do not understand Your grace, it is too big to comprehend. But I stand on Your Word by faith and simply say, thank You. Amen.*

# The Giver

*A Gift from Jesus and the Holy Spirit*

I am the Eternal Giver. I give you life and breath and love.

The only sacrifice that is acceptable to Me is a heart filled with My own love. What you try to bring to Me is not sufficient because it is not holy. Only I can make you holy. I give you My holiness so that what you offer back to Me is an acceptable offering. You must accept My righteousness to become righteous. In order to be able to give anything back to Me, you must first accept what I give.

By accepting My gifts of holiness and righteousness, your life will begin to overflow into service for others who need My help. Just do not forget that all of your goodness comes from My willingness to give it to you. Praise is good when I am in it, but you can never give Me anything that is worthy of praise. I alone am worthy of praise. Take My goodness and then be good. Take My righteousness and then live holy. Take My love and destroy the hate around you.

I am your Giver, the Giver of life. Life from My hand is true, abundant life. Live in My giving and you will never lack anything. Bear My heart that I have given you and see the living results that flow from it. I will never leave you or forsake you.

Accept what I am giving. My peace I give to you. This is not the world's peace. No! My peace surpasses understanding. It flows from Me directly; you cannot generate it or produce it on your own. Never forget that I am the Peace Giver.

Stop trying to produce something in your life that can only come from Me. I am giving it away freely; you cannot use your meager resources to produce what is already free! I will never give you a bad gift. I am the perfect Gift Giver!

# Is Your Faith Full?

*We can go on from day to day, knowing that He loves us and not worrying about our salvation. (The way to salvation is righteousness by faith, not righteousness by worry!)*

C. Mervyn Maxwell, Tell It to the World

Living behind bars is difficult, but living on death row is something completely different. The men who live on death row are forced to live in even greater confinement than other prisoners. They are not allowed to go outside in the sunshine or associate with other men. For twenty-three of the twenty-four hours in a day, they stay locked up in a tiny cell year after year.

One of these men, Dwight J. Loving, had his sentence commuted by President Obama in January 2017 after spending twenty-eight years on death row. For the first time in almost three decades, this man was able to fellowship with other believers.

> Faith is a strange concept for most people, even for Christians, because it means something so radical. You see, faith is a common fisherman stepping over the side of his boat expecting the water to hold him up.

Personally, I love Brother Loving! He always has a smile on his face, and no matter what is going on, he will stop and greet you. Every week in church, Brother Loving asks the chaplain to pray that the men on death row will come to know Jesus, or if they already do, that they will remain faithful. The other day, I found Brother Loving in the hallway carrying a small piece of paper that he was reading. I asked what he was reading and found that he was memorizing Scripture. This is called faithfulness.

Faith is a strange concept for most people, even for Christians, because it means something so radical. You see, faith is a common fisherman stepping over the side of his boat expecting the water to hold him up. For most people, walking on water is impossible, "but with God all things are possible" (Matt. 19:26). When a person is full of faith, he or she is going to appear to be a fool to most people. I mean, everyone knows that unless water is frozen, you cannot walk on it, right? That is a fact, but it is the opposite of faith.

Faith does not work by following human logic or common sense. Faith asks *What does God say?* and then it follows His Word without doubting. Faith even goes so far as to thank God for what He promises long before receiving it. Most people do not say thank you until *after* getting a gift, but faith-filled people are not like most people.

Faith-filled people know that "without faith it is impossible to please Him [God], for he who comes to God must believe that He is [that He exists] and that He is a rewarder of those who seek Him" (Heb. 11:6). God rewards people who believe in Him, and He rewards those who are full of faith.

Peter did not let a little logic stop him from stepping out in faith and trusting Jesus. He trusted Jesus with his life. Most people are not like Peter. They are staying in the boat, where it is logical and safe, but most people miss out on experiencing miracles by refusing to step out in faith.

Yes, those miracles come with trials (Peter fell into the water) but for faith-filled Christians, this is how they build up endurance. **"Consider it all joy, my brethren, when you encounter various trials, knowing that the testing of your faith produces endurance. And let endurance have its perfect result, so that you may be perfect and complete, lacking in nothing" (James 1:2–4).** Faith endures whatever trial it encounters because faith believes in God.

A faith-filled person does not doubt when asking God for wisdom because God's Word says, **"But if any of you lacks wisdom, let him ask of God, who gives to all generously and without reproach, and it *will be* given to him" (James 1:5, italics mine).** I wonder how many people read that verse and think, *Yeah, but* …. That simple word "but" will negate the whole process! People are very good at doubting, but the Scripture states a person "must *ask in faith without any doubting*, for the one who doubts is like the surf of the sea, driven and tossed by the wind. For that man ought not to expect that he will receive anything from the Lord, being a double-minded man, unstable in all his ways" (James 1:6–8, italics mine). Somehow we need to settle it, like concrete in our minds, that what God says is true. We need to be full of faith in His Word.

You might be thinking, *Well, I am not like Peter. My faith is too small.* I am reminded of someone else whose resources were small. But what little she had, she entrusted fully to God and used whole heartedly for Him.

Jesus sat in the temple observing how people put money into the treasury. He watched rich people as they proudly deposited large sums, loudly letting their money fall into the collection box. They were very proud of themselves, but Jesus was not impressed. One after another, these rich braggarts flaunted their generosity and piousness. Then, out of the corner of His eye, He spotted her. She was standing in the shadows, too embarrassed to be seen by the others; her gift was so insignificant. As a widow, she was very poor, and all she had to give were two small copper coins. She quietly slipped them into the collection box. **"Calling His disciples to Him, He said to them, 'Truly I say to you, this poor widow put in more than all the contributors to the treasury; for they all put in out of their surplus, but she, out of her poverty, put in all she owned, all she had to live on'" (Mark 12:43–44).**

I would like to encourage you today—*put all that you have into the treasury, and live a life that is full of faith. Why not step out of the boat?* Yes, you might look like a fool when you stop watching certain movies, throw away all of your porn, or stop cursing. Sure, people might say you are crazy when you smile at them or talk about Jesus, but so what? Faith is an *action* verb!

Do you know why I love Brother Loving so much? Because he is a faith-filled person, my brother in Christ! Even though he could be bitter and angry, locked up for the rest of his life in prison, instead he smiles. Jesus is in his heart. I know that wherever he goes he will be faithful to Jesus.

When we see life through the eyes of faith, we see the water turn into a sidewalk! Turn to Jesus, bring your two cents (all that you have, however little that may be), and by faith find His mercy, compassion, and forgiveness. If Brother Loving can do it, you can too! (See Appendix 2, page 61.)

*Father, teach me how to trust you by faith. I believe without doubting that You are my Provider, Strength and Shield. By faith, I bring these two cents to You. Help me to get out of the boat of fear and do the impossible by faith. I rejoice in my trials knowing that I am learning to endure. Help me be faithful. Amen.*

# The Widow's Mite

*From Jesus*

You must be all in before I can bless you fully. Many who claim to follow Me are shortsighted in this area. My heart is broken when you don't trust Me enough to let Me be your solution. Do you love Me? If so, keep My commandments.

People will tell you to just follow your heart, but your heart is deceitful and wicked. When the widow gave her gift to Me it was more than her just following her heart. No, she was fully surrendered, obediently trusting in My ability to provide outside of what she could see or feel. It is not enough to just *feel* compelled to follow Me. Feelings are deceptive. Instead, follow Me in obedience no matter how it feels.

I am calling you to a higher experience in your walk with Me. Let's go beyond feelings to a *real* relationship with ups and downs and even sadness and heartbreak. What you will find in the end will be ultimate delivery and redemption. Are you ready for this level of commitment? This is a true Christian walk with Me. Understand, as we walk together the path will seem to become more narrow and dangerous. You will look down and see everyone else walking on what looks like a much easier road—but remember, *that road* is the road to death and destruction.

When others see what you are doing they will mock you and even look at you as pitiful, but in truth they are the ones to pity. You must love those who mock you. Maybe they will be won to Me through your steadfastness and love toward them. I am not a respecter of persons. Everyone is the same in My sight and all are in need of a Savior.

Humble yourself. Give Me everything first. Like the widow, your efforts may seem small and insignificant to you, but you will see how much I can do with even the smallest offering of faith.

# Am I Poor Enough?

*We also need to realize that God so loved the world that Jesus died
for people we don't even like.*

Chris Blake, *Searching for a God to Love*

People who really love others in the way that Jesus told His disciples to love are very special people. Great compassion emanates from their pores! Their senses are highly attuned to the cry of the heart, the need of a neighbor, or any other gesture of kindness that they can give to help others. A follower of Jesus never ignores a broken person. Time, money, and energy are all gifts these saints see as resources to help, uplift, support, or encourage people who are in need. For these disciples, loving service is their greatest joy. They value others more than they value themselves. This is called being poor in spirit.

It is never above one of these humble servants of Christ to reach out and help or heal whomever they contact. You see, a person humble enough to acknowledge his or her own spiritual poverty will be quick to look past the spiritual lack in others. People who look and act like Jesus tend to move toward impoverished souls and nurture relationships with the hurting.

Many people carry terrible wounds they hide deep inside, but some just wear their pain right on their faces. I remember the drastic contrast I felt between the outside world and the cold atmosphere of prison when I first encountered other inmates, some of whom had been locked away from society for many years. They wore a look of despair, gloom, and darkness. A strange sadness seemed to permeate the air around them—a palpable sadness.

I felt a piercing chill run through my spine as I watched face after face pass by, each wearing the same expression. Fear gripped me as I moved past these walking shadows, these men filled with ruin. The haunting thought, *Will I look like that after a few years?* seemed to jeer at my apparent misfortune and swirl around me in ever-growing levels of darkness. I felt myself slipping, falling end-over-end, into a deep trench of despair as the heavy metal doors slammed behind me, locking me into the hopeless chasm of oblivion.

> The wonderful thing about being in darkness is that the tiniest light shines very bright. In my desperation, in the middle of my deep despair, a voluntary kindness brought me overwhelming joy.

After two weeks in prison, I ran out of toothpaste. The tiny travel-size tube I received on my arrival was gone. I knew that I would have to wait two more weeks before getting the chance to order a larger tube from the "Health and Comfort Sheet." A panic rose within me. It sounds like a tiny thing, but everything becomes magnified to a new inmate in prison. I mentioned my problem to one of the other men, mostly venting my concern. That night, I reached for my toothpaste tube expecting to squeeze out the last remaining bit; instead, I found more than half of the tube full of toothpaste! That man, in a gesture of genuine kindness, had filled my toothpaste tube from his own supply. He never asked me for anything in return, even after I offered. He was simply happy to help me. That was an incredible gift to me.

The wonderful thing about being in darkness is that the tiniest light shines very bright. In my desperation, in the middle of my deep despair, a voluntary kindness brought me overwhelming joy. I wept over that tiny tube with tears of relief and gratitude. Knowing that there was at least one other man like that in this prison helped me know that I would be okay.

Ellen G. White writes about this perfectly in her powerful book, *The Greatest Sermon Ever Preached*:

> The golden rule is the principle of true courtesy, and its truest illustration is seen in the life and character of Jesus. Oh, what rays of softness and beauty shone forth in the daily life of our Saviour! What sweetness flowed from His very presence! The same spirit will be revealed in His children. Those with whom Christ dwells will be surrounded with a divine atmosphere. Their white robes of purity will be fragrant with perfume from the garden of the Lord. Their faces will reflect light from His, brightening the path for stumbling and weary feet. (p. 135)

Jesus said, **"Let your light shine before men" (Matt. 5:16).** Sometimes I don't feel like my light is shining very brightly, but if I am transparent, *His* light will shine through me. I remember how I felt when I was given that toothpaste and I know that a small gesture can change everything. God is looking for people who are poor in *their* spirit and rich in *His* Spirit. "*Theirs* is the kingdom of heaven"

(Matt. 5:3, italics mine). These are the ones who fulfill the Lord's Prayer, **"Your kingdom come. Your will be done, on earth as it is in heaven" (Matt. 6:10).** These are the ones showing true mercy, compassion, and forgiveness.

*Father, Make me poor in my spirit and rich in Yours I pray. In Jesus' name, Amen.*

# My Love

## *Words from the Great I AM*

Go out with humility and be My voice. I will empower your lack and fill you with My abilities. Nothing that you do on your own will work—but with Me, you cannot fail. I do not want your scraps. I want your all. Don't expect to succeed by partial obedience. I need it all. I am your Provider and have all of the resources that you could ever need. I have the energy, the money, and the time, but you must bring yourself to Me. I have always been there, but many times you tried to do it without My help and you failed.

There will always be obstacles, but I am the mover of them, not you. Do you trust Me enough to move them for you?

*I give you my mountains, God.*

Good, because I am ready to start moving the impossibilities out of the way in your life. Remember, I am the Way. I already blazed this path for you when I took your mountains on the cross. I love you enough; you don't need anything or anyone else.

The enemy has attempted to destroy the evidence of My love in this world, but I will use you to show it off in his face. You are going to shine in My love. This is how much I love you. The greatest gift that I can give you is My eternal love.

Without My love, you are nothing and cannot stand before Me, because I AM LOVE. My love expands so rapidly, there is no way to contain it. That is why the universe must always expand outward, because My love is that immense.

# Why Don't We Pray to Carl?

*And now you can travel around this world and visit countries where 75 years ago the people were cannibals, and today these same people have been transformed by the gospel from raw, heathen, savage cannibals to loving, tenderhearted Christians. The gospel has been carried to every nation on the earth, during the lifetime of men and women living today.*

Evangelist M.L. Venden, *Along the Sawdust Trail*

Here in prison, I have met some of the most faithful Christians I have ever known in my whole life. It never ceases to amaze me, the irony of it!

At work, each day, two Christian brothers join me in the morning to pray before we begin our workday. We usually share a few encouraging thoughts with one another and then ask for God's protection over ourselves and the men who work around us. We believe that these prayers shield us (and the unbelievers around us), bringing peace into a volatile work place—a shop filled with dangerous equipment and quick tempers. Prayer like this is called intercession.

> As he walked away, I thought about his question. *Why don't we pray to Carl?* As I pondered this idea, I began to picture what the gospel according to Carl is, or more accurately, is *not*.

Last week as we gathered to pray, a fellow worker approached our group with a question. "I know you all believe, but why do you pray to Jesus? It's just a *name*, right? Why can't you pray to Carl?" I thought he was joking, but he insisted, "No, I'm serious. Why does it have to be Jesus?"

I told him that the Bible says His name "is above every other name" (Phil. 2:9).

He responded, "That's just *a* book, one of *many* books."

As he walked away, I thought about his question. *Why don't we pray to Carl?* As I pondered this idea, I began to picture what the gospel according to Carl is, or more accurately, is *not*. To begin with, I have never heard the gospel of Carl preached to me anywhere I have gone in my forty years of life. There are no faithful followers of Carl devoting time, money, and energy to spread his word. Moreover, there is no written testimony of Carl's life, telling of his miracles and works of kindness to the poor and needy. Nowhere have I ever listened to the reading of Carl's word, written by those who saw him rise from the dead and who then gave up their whole lives to tell what they had seen and heard, exclaiming to the whole world that they had walked with God in the flesh.

I further wondered who in their right mind would confront demons in Carl's name and command them to leave. The thought itself is absurd. The gospel of Carl is so ludicrous, one would probably be committed to an institution for professing it; then again, on second thought, maybe not these days!

In contrast, throughout history billions have experienced new life in Jesus. In Jesus' name, the sick have been healed, the dead raised to life, and the worst sinners transformed. *Is* it just another name? Why do demons become intimidated when *His* name is invoked? Why is *His* name used as a curse word and not Carl's? Could it be that His *name* holds incredible power and authority? Could it be that Jesus really *was* God in the flesh—a Man who really *did* love His creation?

Is it possible that He really *did* leave us His Word so that we could get to know the character attributes of our Creator? No book in the history of the world has ever been so hated, so powerful, and as fully untouchable as the Bible. Kings have tried to destroy it, geniuses have tried to discredit it, and whole nations have banned it; yet it continues to speak. The most humble child can understand it, and wise men remain baffled by it. It is the Word. It stands as a testament to a God who never changes. Jesus said, **"Heaven and earth will pass away, but My words will not pass away" (Matt. 24:35).** Two thousand years have passed, and those words are still here, but where are Carl's words?

Jesus spoke His words confidently because He knew who He was and why He was here. **"I came forth from the Father and have come into the world; I am leaving the world again and going to the Father" (John 16:28).** He came to Earth for one reason, and that reason was to save you and me.

Deep down, each of us know that we are sinners and God is real, but many of us are stubborn.

> **"And just as they did not see fit to acknowledge God any longer, God gave them over to a depraved mind, to do those things which are not proper, being filled with all unrighteousness, wickedness, greed, evil; full of envy, murder, strife, deceit, malice; they are gossips, slanderers, haters of God, insolent, arrogant, boastful, inventors of evil, disobedient to parents, without understanding, untrustworthy, unloving, unmerciful; and although they know**

the ordinance of God, that those who practice such things are worthy of death, they not only do the same, but also give hearty approval to those who practice them" (Rom. 1:28–32).

The reason people hate the Bible so much is because the Bible exposes who people really are, sinners in need of a Savior. All of us are guilty of at least one of those faults in the list.

We just need to be honest (transparent) with ourselves and say, "Jesus, I need Your help." The good news is Jesus lives to intercede for us. **"Therefore He is able also to save forever those who draw near to God through Him, since He always lives to make intercession for them" (Heb. 7:25).** That's something Carl can't do.

You see, the reason I pray to Jesus every morning, and not to Carl, is because Jesus is *my intercessor*. I bring Him my fears and worries, and in their place, He gives me joy and peace.

Since I want to be like Jesus, with my Christian coworkers I choose to intercede on behalf of other sinners who need Him too. The unbelievers around us might mock or shun us for it, but Jesus told us (in advance) to expect that. In fact, every day Christians are murdered by people who hate Jesus. Was someone murdered today for believing in Carl? Nope.

**"We are from God; he who knows God listens to us; he who is not from God does not listen to us. By this we know the spirit of truth and the spirit of error" (1 John 4:6).** Listen, Jesus loves you. Jesus died for you. Jesus rose from the dead. Jesus now intercedes for you. Jesus is coming back for you. Carl … yeah, he's not for me. Only Jesus gives me mercy, compassion, and forgiveness!

*Jesus, thank You for being God. I believe in You and Your everlasting Word. Thank you for interceding for me and taking all my sin and shame so that I could be free. I love You. Amen.*

# Knowledge

*Wisdom from the Father*

I created all of My children with a certain kind of intellect. When used for selfish gain, this intellect is perverted and darkened by the enemy. Instead, I want My children to have knowledge. This must come from Me and not from your universities. Learning is good, but the search for the deeper understanding of My will in your life will increase your knowledge in spiritual strength. This is what you were created for—to know Me.

To begin to know Me you must let go of what you think you know already. If you want Me to do amazing things in your life, you must let go of your own preconceived ideas and thoughts of who you think I am. I am bigger than that! I outwit your wittiest thoughts and I surpass your biggest imaginations. I am your God whom you cannot contain. I move like the wind which you cannot direct.

Submit to Me for power and direction in your life. Pride, stubbornness, and self-sufficiency prevent Me from granting you strength, courage, and power. My children should be equipped with the best and strongest attributes to withstand the trials of life. Real strength is not in numbers but in a knowledge of the truth. My Word is truth and it is powerful like a two-edged sword.

True knowledge is love that surpasses human understanding. I died for you so that you would be able to ask Me for knowledge. I love you, my child. Just remember, your intellect is useless without My knowledge filling your mind. Know Me, learn how to hear My voice. Listen as I direct you and your knowledge will increase exponentially.

# Am I Really a Felon?

*The rulers derided Him, the soldiers mocked, and even the thieves that were hanging there on either side of Him expressed doubt.... the multitude that passed by joined in reviling the Savior. In their ignorance, they thought that they had made a point and an argument. They thought that the silence of Christ and His apparent weakness proved that His claims were false, and that He was not truly the Son of God. But you and I know that it was because of love and pity that He hung there and bore all that abuse, and stayed on the cross when He might have come down.*

W.D. Frazee, *Crisis at the Close*

"Lock them up and throw away the key! Those worthless pieces of trash don't deserve to see the light of day ever again!" Words like these are spoken every day about people like me who sit condemned behind bars in America.

Some of the harshest words come from people who call themselves children of God, a.k.a. Christians. For many Christians mercy, compassion, and forgiveness are not strong suits. (As a professing Christian, my heart aches even admitting this. However, transparency leads us to freedom, so let's be clear.) The good traits seem to surface most when Christians are surrounded by people like themselves. It is easy to be nice to people we like. The real test happens when we encounter people we do not like. How do we talk about those we consider to be *real* criminals? If someone has clearly done us wrong, are we quick to point out that person's faults and insult them? Do we feel powerful in our superiority? That is called self-righteousness.

Consider Jesus. He was superior in every way to every person He met, but His response to mistreatment was different than ours. He hung on the Cross unjustly condemned as a criminal, yet His response was a prayer for his tormenters. **"Father, forgive them, because they do not know what they are doing" (Luke 23:34, CSB).**

In contrast, these self-righteous church leaders who claimed to love and adore God, condescendingly mocked Him and spit on Jesus—who was God. What a contradiction! How shameful!

Jesus said that the way we treat "the least of these" is the way we are treating Him (Matt. 25:40, 45). Who are the *least* in our society today? Think about that for a moment. Who comes to mind? Is it the homeless person you see every day at the stop sign downtown? What about the poor woman at the grocery store who has too little in her cart? Perhaps it is a person in prison, in trouble, or maybe living in shame. The person or group who comes to mind is the person or group to help. Keep in mind—the homeless, the poor, the prisoner—all represent Jesus. He said He was each of these. If we fail to act, Jesus will say, **"Depart from Me .... Truly I say to you, to the extent that you did *not* do it to one of the least of these, you did *not* do it to *Me*"** (Matt. 25:41, 45, italics mine). This should be our wakeup call. The alarm is blaring!

As Jesus hung there, innocent of all wrongdoing, one voice called out above the taunts and cries of the others. It was the voice of a criminal, a truly guilty felon, who did not deserve a bit of compassion. At *his* trial, his accusers were totally warranted when they said, "Crucify him! Society is much safer with this thief off the streets!" However, something happened when this felon met Jesus. He called out His name.

*"Jesus."*

*Jesus* is the Greek version of the Hebrew name *Joshua* which translates, "Jehovah saved." Today Jehovah God is still saving everyone who calls out to Him in faith by the name of Jesus. Every undeserving sinner has the right to cry out in his or her pain, heartache, or sadness, and say, *"Jesus, remember me."* This is not just a common request. Calling out for Jehovah to "remember me" was a Jewish tradition, a request invoking God to bless His people and honor His covenant (see Judges 16:28 and 1 Sam. 1:11). Therefore, in this request the thief recognized Jesus as God and expected help from Him.

Here was the least of these, a convicted felon, crying out to his Creator for a blessing that he knew he did not deserve. However, he *did* recognize his need! Now it should be obvious here, but the point is that it is usually the poor, the outcast, and the marginalized who actually reach the heart of Jesus with their cries. He knows their deep desire and longing for His help. While the self-righteous stand there condemning the felons, the felons find salvation. In perfect irony, Jesus loves sinners and saves them, while the self-righteous people are rejecting Jesus by hating the felons *they* call "lost" and "worthless." Jesus must be so sad seeing this kind of self-righteousness in action when He has made it possible for *all* to find mercy, compassion, and forgiveness from Him.

The inconvenient truth is that we are *all* felons before God. **"All have sinned and fall short of the glory of God" (Rom. 3:23).** All of us are undeserving of grace, but Jesus gives freedom only to people who ask for it. When they ask, how eagerly He responds as He did to the thief, *"Truly,"* which is *amen* in Hebrew (His way of affirming!). He is happy to respond to such a request! How God's heart rejoices when a sinner's heart repents! Jesus said to that felon, *"Truly ... you shall be with Me"* (Luke 23:43).*

Is there anything better than to be with God truly and to have His assurance today? Today is the day of salvation. He loves you more than you love yourself. This is great news! In fact, it's fantastic news! It's truly *Paradise!*

*Father, forgive those of us who condemn others. We, too, are felons before you. Show us a new vision, a new perspective on what it means to be a Christian. I love you, Jesus. Thank You for your mercy, compassion, and forgiveness that is available today. Amen.*

---

*Because of Jesus' statement in John 20:17, many scholars believe that translators should have placed the comma *after* "today" in Luke 23:43 so that it reads "Truly I say to you today, you shall be with Me in Paradise." This emphasizes the hope Christ offers amidst the apparent hopeless circumstances "today" instead of designating a time of arrival in Paradise.

# The Challenge

*A Reminder from Jesus: Our Mission*

When you look at My creation and the work of My hands (other people) and say that My creation is not good, you dishonor Me. *Sin* is not good, but My *creation* is good. Know the difference when you speak to people. Otherwise, you will be sinning against Me. As you have done it to the least of these, you have done it unto Me.

Pursue the things that make peace and build one another up. This is My commandment: love one another. Forgetting this brings division and destruction. Satan is the one who comes to kill, steal, and destroy. Who is your Father? Choose today whom you will serve.

My kingdom reaches farther than you can comprehend. What you see in others is not what I see in others. Sinners are *very* precious to Me. I eat at their houses, because of how grateful they are to have Me there. Are sinners grateful to have *you* around? Do they *know* when they look at you that you love them, or do they feel discarded? This is how you can tell if I am really dwelling in your heart; My love will directly love them through you.

I am looking for a heart change in My church today. There is too much shunning and not enough compassion. Let Me handle the devil and his plans. You focus on loving. Love with abandon. Love with mercy. Love with forgiveness in your hearts, knowing that I loved you through your stubbornness and selfishness. How else will they see Me? How else will they find Me? You are My representative on earth.

You are My "Sermon on the Mount" today. Go and sin no more. Be pure of heart; be merciful; be peacemakers; and you will be blessed. Follow Me, and I will make you fishers of men. Go and show My church what that looks like. Go show them how much I love you.

# Pardon Me, Can You See?

*We must never forget the fact that as long as we live in this land of the enemy,*
*Satan and his spirit associates will do everything possible to make us feel terrible.*
*They may even torture the minds of some of us as they did to John the Baptist.*
*If he had listened to his feelings while in prison, he would have missed out on eternal life.*

Roger J. Morneau, *The Incredible Power of Prayer*

Of all the chapters in this book, this one is the hardest for me to write. Not because it contains bad news. On the contrary, it has the best news of all. No, this chapter is difficult for me because I know that some of you have read this whole book, and still you do not understand its meaning for you personally. This is not an insult to your intellect, but a revealing of your spiritual condition.

Paul says that if the gospel is veiled, "it is veiled to those who are perishing, in whose case the god of this world [the devil] has blinded the minds of the unbelieving so that they might not see the light of the gospel of the glory of Christ, who is the image of God" (2 Cor. 4:3, 4). It is sad, but the devil has blindfolded many people so that they cannot see the wonderful love and goodness of God revealed in Jesus. The only way to remove this blindfold is by coming to Jesus. The veil "is removed in Christ" (2 Cor. 3:14). This veil is called spiritual blindness.

> I am about to share with you something that millions of people do not know. These three words might change your life forever; to a prisoner, these words are freeing.

Day after day, I walk past men here in this prison who have no idea that they are blind. Of course, this problem is not confined to prison. It is a universal problem! I am about to share with you something that millions of people do not know. These three words might change your life forever; to a prisoner, these words are freeing. I hope that you are sitting down for these because they are a real bombshell! Here they are: You. Are. Forgiven. Yep, even right now as you sit there dumbstruck, reading my lousy attempt to give you the best news you ever received in your whole life! You are forgiven.

Pardon is available. Will you accept it?

You see, two thousand years ago, as Jesus hung there dying on that cruel cross he said, *"Father, forgive them"* (Luke 23:34). Yes, even while you were out in the world living in sin, being selfish, taking care of number one, hating God, and openly rejecting His love for you; while you were ignoring that persistent inner voice warning you not to do those things you were doing, God was saying, "You are *already* forgiven." The crazy part was that you had no idea He was saying that about you two thousand years ago. I mean, how could you have known? You were not even born yet! **"For while we were still helpless, at the right time Christ died for the ungodly.... God demonstrates His own love toward us, in that while we were yet sinners, Christ died for us" (Rom. 5:6, 8).** Yes, He pardoned you. He removed your guilt and shame. The Father accepted the Lamb of God as an offering in your place. On that day, Jesus took upon Himself every sin you ever committed, are committing, or will commit. On that day, Jesus set you free. You could not free yourself. You were helpless, but His love pardoned you nonetheless.

Still, some of you are reading these words and they mean nothing to you. Knowing this breaks my heart. Here is the bottom line: **"No one can say, 'Jesus is [my] Lord,' except by the Holy Spirit" (1 Cor. 12:3).** In other words, it is the Holy Spirit's job to change your heart, mind, and inclinations. He is the One who causes you to fall in love with Jesus. Many will say, "Lord, Lord," but few people actually want Him to have His way in every aspect of their lives (see Matt. 7:21). This is the crux of the matter. Most of us, if we would be bravely transparent, could name things in our lives to fill in this blank: "I have prioritized _____ over Jesus."

But most of us are not that honest or brave, even with ourselves. If this rings true in your life, then ask the Holy Spirit to open your eyes so you will be a blind prisoner to sin no longer. Jesus said,

> *"For everyone who asks, receives;* and he who seeks, finds; and to him who knocks, it will be opened. Now suppose one of you fathers is asked by his son for a fish; he will not give him a snake instead of a fish, will he? Or if he is asked for an egg, he will not give him a scorpion, will he? If you then, being evil, know how to give good gifts to your children, *how much more will your heavenly Father give the Holy Spirit to those who ask Him?"* (Luke 11:10–13, italics mine).

Do you still doubt that your heavenly Father is a good father? **"Consider the ravens, for they neither sow nor reap; they have no storeroom nor barn, and yet God feeds them; how much more valuable you are than the birds!" (Luke 12:24). "Do not be afraid ... for your Father has chosen gladly to give you the kingdom" (verse 32).**

> "Now when they heard this, they were pierced to the heart, and said ..., 'Brethren, what shall we do?' Peter said to them, 'Repent, and each of you be baptized in the name of Jesus Christ for the forgiveness of your sins; and you will receive the gift of the Holy Spirit. For the promise is for you and for your children and for all who are far off, as many as the Lord our God will call to Himself .... So then, those who had received his word were baptized." (Acts 2:37–39, 41).

Do you hear Him calling you? I assure you that He is patient and does not want you to miss out. **"The Lord is not slow about His promise, as some count slowness, but is patient toward you, not wishing for any to perish but for all to come to repentance" (2 Pet. 3:9).** To repent means to turn around and go the other way. Turn away from everything that distracts you and takes your eyes off Jesus. Turn away from your old life, "seeing that His divine power has granted to us everything pertaining to life and godliness, through the true knowledge of Him who called us ... so that by them you may become partakers of the divine nature, having escaped the corruption that is in the world by lust" (2 Pet. 1:3, 4).

It is not too late. He is calling you today. Jesus has already forgiven you, but like anyone else who forgives, He is waiting to see *whether you will accept* His forgiveness. Think about a pardon—like forgiveness, a pardon is never forced; it is only offered as a gift. In the same way, the beauty of His forgiveness is that it is free. You cannot pay for it or earn it by being perfect enough. You just reach out and accept it saying, "Thank you!" Then believe that you are forgiven, and you will be! Today my friend, you just received the greatest gift ever given—forgiveness for all your sins!

> "Amazing grace! how sweet the sound,
> That saved a wretch like me!
> I once was lost, but now am found,
> Was blind, but now I see."
> (John Newton, "Amazing Grace")

Now that's what I call mercy, compassion, and forgiveness!

*Father, it is my deepest desire to know You and Jesus even better. Please send Your Holy Spirit and fill my life today with Your presence. I want Your forgiveness, so I say thank You for what You already did for me. I accept Your wonderful free gift—Your pardon. Show me how to live for You, and walk in Your eternal life. Amen.*

# Don't Worry I've Got This

*From God—the One in Control*

Take every thought captive. Your inner man must become a prisoner to Me with no possibility of parole! Your thoughts are always subject to whoever is controlling you.

Ask Me for spiritual hearing aids to hear My voice more clearly, since I am always speaking to you, but you rarely hear Me. The reason is because you are overanalyzing things in your head and this is blocking you from hearing My words. When I tell you to pray without ceasing, I am not exaggerating. Praying this way is the opposite of overthinking and worrying about things.

Enoch was like this, and once he found Me he did not let go! Do you know what I can accomplish through you in this way? Everything! I want to consume your time, energy, pleasure, pain, troubles, and then bring you joy that you could not find anywhere else—and I know you have searched everywhere.

But My thoughts are not your thoughts, and My ways are not your ways. My way is perfect! Are you perfect?

*No.*

But in Me you are. Every person who desires to become My son or daughter ought to wear the robe that I provide. If you come to the wedding wearing your own clothes (your own goodness) you cannot stay with Me. I cannot bless you this way. Remember the prodigal son; the first gift was the robe, which is My righteousness.

Your mind is the battlefield, but the battle is Mine to fight, so you must let Me have your mind if you want to win the war. I have never lost a fight and I am a mighty warrior! Why would you ever tell Me *no*? I am your defender and only chance. Let's do this together and change the world, one thought at a time!

# Conclusion

*When I look at Jesus' perfect example, I say, "I may have a long way to go," but when I look back and see how far He has brought me, it gives me courage. I know He's not done with me yet. If I let Him, He'll finish what He's started in my life, and some day take me home.*

Doug Bachelor, *The Richest Caveman*

I must tell you a very simple truth. I am a humble servant of yours and write these words only to bless you. As the reader, I pray that you find in them a new perspective and a new hope for your future. While I would like to take all of the credit, God is the Author and the Finisher of my faith (see Hebrews 12:2). He wrote the first word in my mind and authored the faith that I have transcribed and shared with you in these pages.

As our Creator, He knows exactly how to produce in us a perfect faith that honors Him. It is simply our job to believe in His perfect work that He performs day by day in our lives. One day He will finish the work He has begun in us and our faith will be made sight. As we look upon His plan in its completion, we will review our lives and exclaim that everything He accomplished in us was perfect. Then we will say, "In You alone, oh God we have found mercy, compassion, and forgiveness."

*God, give me the strength to trust in Your awesome plan of redemption, even during the dark days of imprisonment. No one but You knows the mighty struggle that I face to walk with You by faith through the darkness, but I trust in You completely and ask You to have Your way in my heart so that my faith will more clearly reflect Jesus.*

*You are God, and I am just a man in need of a Savior. You are my Savior, and I know that Your salvation is complete and perfect in its work. Thank You for that. I trust in it with all of my heart.*

*I believe by faith that You are more than able to do the impossible in my life. You can transform this heart to move mountains in the lives of others who are hurting and do not understand Your great goodness. You can use my words to encourage the weak who love You but do not live in Your power by faith.*

*By faith, I will walk in the power of the Holy Spirit and lift up the weak ones who are burdened by the guilt of sin that has overcome them. You have redeemed me to show them that there is hope for the worst of sinners who will trust in You by faith.*

*I am Yours to use as You see fit.*

*Your son*

# Appendix 1

# The Gospel of Carl

The gospel of Carl is not really great, it carries no hope, it brings awful fate.
The name is forgettable and really quite bland, and no one proclaims it all over the land.
The gospel of Carl is terribly weak, and for those who are looking, it is not what they seek.
There is no saving power and no saving grace, the message of Carl falls flat on its face.
No missions are formed proclaiming his word, and when Carl is mentioned, no prayer can be heard.
His name brings no rest to the weary and poor, you won't find him knocking there at your door.
When you are hurting, injured, or sick, Carl can't heal, and he won't solve things quick.
The dead can't be raised in Carl's name, and demons don't flee, they just laugh at the claim.
To put it as bluntly and clear as I can, Carl can't do it because Carl's a man.
If Carl's your god then things won't end well; by following Carl, you'll end up in hell.
Yet there is One, up in heaven above, Who died in our place out of infinite love.
He carried the weight of all of our sin, and now by His Spirit He lives here within.
His name is Jesus and there is no other; He was born in our flesh from a young virgin mother.
He died on a cross so that we could be free, He did it for you, and yes, even for me.
I don't worship Carl; I love Jesus instead. My God is alive—but Carl is dead!

# Appendix 2

# A Prisoner's Testimony

*By Dwight J. Loving*

"God is good! On December 13, 1988, I was arrested and charged with multiple armed robberies, and two murders. I was guilty and felt that I deserved whatever I had coming. It was a horrible feeling then and a horrible memory for me now.

The next month and a half were a blur. In early February, my Article 32 hearings and other hearings began. By this time my thought processes were a little bit less stable. I continued to want to be punished for what I did. But I did not really believe that the death penalty was something that I would get. Not that I didn't deserve it. I simply didn't think it was a possibility. My thoughts were unstable.

The military decided to seek the death penalty and I knew that I deserved it. Had they gone a different route, seeking a penalty of life in prison, I would have felt the same way. I suppose I was anxious to be punished for my crimes. The trial started in late February 1989 and ended on the third of April. The judge read the verdict aloud and I felt, *I deserve it; that is that.*

There are a great many things that have happened between now and then, There is literally not a day that goes by that I am not praying for the families and loved ones of the two men that I murdered. It hurts me that I murdered them and I know that my hurt cannot begin to touch the pain the families must feel to this day. I wrote about my feelings of anguish because I was lost. I did not know what to do with myself as I awaited my death. I embraced nude magazines and books describing all kinds of nasty stuff. It got so bad that at one point I had naked photos all over my walls and along my floor so that I could see naked women from any position in my cell. I was a mess.

I considered myself a Christian at the time. But I could not break the hold that the naked women—and really my lustful desires—had on me. I know now that the reason I couldn't stop is because I did not want to. I am ashamed of the way that I used to be, but at the time I felt I was alright. That is what I thought at the time.

In January 1999, the Lord convicted me and I got rid of all the nude magazines. I continued to seek magazines with beautiful women. Only now they had clothes on. I know, I know that lusting is lusting whether they are clothed or not. It took time, but I threw them all out. June 1999 I was baptized and happy. From that moment until now I have had a joy that is unsurpassed. I thank God every day for His grace and mercy.

President Obama commuted my sentence to life without parole. I had been on death row from the third of April 1989 until January 2017. I was ready to see our Lord but it is clear that He has other plans for me. I clearly left out a lot of things that I have been through while on death row. Think of being locked down for a least twenty-three hours a day for nearly twenty-eight years and you will begin to imagine my thoughts on it.

God has sustained me and continues to sustain me. He has brought many wonderful people into my life. There are those in the administration, cadre, and fellow prisoners that have been, and continue to be, a blessing. God is GOOD!"

# Appendix 3

# Prayer 101

Some of us really want to pray but the words are hard to formulate and the format seems hard to understand. Below is a simple template to help you jump start your prayer life right now. Practice these steps until they become your own. This is only a suggestion, but one that has worked for me. I pray that you have a closer, sweeter walk of your own with Jesus.

*"Draw near to God and He will draw near to you." James 4:8*

**1. Offer praise and adoration to His name and give thanks to Him.**
*I praise You Father for _____. You are worthy of all adoration and praise. Thank You for _____ in my life.*

**2. Acknowledge your sin and separation from Him.**
*Father, I have sinned before You and grieved the Holy Spirit by _____.*

**3. Repent for thoughts, words, or deeds which are blocking you from Him.**
*I confess to You today that I thought/said/did _____ and I knew it was wrong. Please forgive me for these sins.*

**4. Thank Him for giving you the gift of forgiveness and for covering you with Christ's righteousness.**
*Thank You for being a merciful God. You have promised me that when I confess my sin You forgive it. I know that You have already forgiven me, and I accept the blood of Jesus as my covering right now for my sin. Thank You for making me righteous in Christ.*

**5. Claim the blood of Jesus over any person or situation that is bothering you and ask the Holy Spirit to overrule in their life and provide salvation.**
*Jesus, I further ask that You cover _____ with forgiveness through Your blood. Please send Your Holy Spirit to overrule in _____ 's life.*

**6. Pray for them to receive heavenly love, joy, and peace; ask for the godly attributes of longsuffering, gentleness, and goodness to cover them.**
*Father, I humbly ask You to pour out in abundant measure over _____ Your heavenly love, heavenly joy, and heavenly peace. And because I know how wonderful and good You are, I ask You to cover _____ with longsuffering, gentleness, and goodness, too.*

**7. Pray the prayer in step six for yourself, also.**
*Father, I need an abundance of Your heavenly love, joy, and peace, too. And please cover me with longsuffering, gentleness, and goodness also.*

**8. Ask God to remove all pride and self-sufficiency and to clothe you with His robe of righteousness.**
*Father, even if it is difficult for me, I ask You to humble me so that I can more accurately represent You in my life. I ask for Your righteousness to cover me today.*

**9. Believe and claim His provision for you, then listen for His voice, taking as long as you need.**
*I believe that You have already done the work on my behalf. Thank You! Is there anything You want me to know? I will wait quietly for You now, Holy Spirit.*

**10. Thank Him again for what He has done for you and give Him the highest praise.**
*Thank You Father again for _____. I submit everything I am before You. I give You all my heart and all my praise. Jesus I praise You for _____. I offer this prayer to You as an offering today. Amen.*

Author's note: I have been blessed by Roger Morneau's books on prayer and highly recommend them. Some of the above points are adapted from his materials.

# Bibliography

Morneau, Roger J. *Charmed by Darkness*, Nampa, ID: Pacific Press, 2015.

———. *Incredible Answers to Prayer*, Hagerstown, MD: Review and Herald Publ. Assn., 1990.

———. *The Incredible Power of Prayer*, Hagerstown, MD: Review and Herald Publ. Assn., 1997.

———. *More Incredible Answers to Prayer*, Hagerstown, MD: Review and Herald Publ. Assn., 1993.

———. *A Trip Into the Supernatural*, Hagerstown, MD: Review and Herald Publ. Assn., 1999.

———. *When You Need Incredible Answers to Prayer*, Hagerstown, MD: Review and Herald Publ. Assn., 1995.

White, Ellen G. *The Greatest Sermon Ever Preached*, Nampa, ID: Pacific Press, 2015.

**TEACH Services, Inc.**
P U B L I S H I N G
www.TEACHServices.com • (800) 367-1844

We invite you to view the complete
selection of titles we publish at:
**www.TEACHServices.com**

We encourage you to write us
with your thoughts about this,
or any other book we publish at:
**info@TEACHServices.com**

TEACH Services' titles may be purchased in
bulk quantities for educational, fund-raising,
business, or promotional use.
**bulksales@TEACHServices.com**

Finally, if you are interested in seeing
your own book in print, please contact us at:
**publishing@TEACHServices.com**
We are happy to review your manuscript at no charge.